MIDDLE EAST LEADERS™

GAMAL ABDEL NASSER

Sam Witte

The Rosen Publishing Group, Inc.,
New York

Published in 2004 by The Rosen Publishing Group, Inc.
29 East 21st Street, New York, NY 10010

Library of Congress Cataloging-in-Publication Data

Witte, Sam.
Gamal Abdel Nasser/ by Sam Witte.— 1st ed.
        p. cm. — (Middle East leaders)
Summary: Examines the life and leadership skills of Egyptian
president Gamal Abdel Nasser, who led the revolt that overthrew
King Faruk in 1952 and established Egypt as a republic.
Includes bibliographical references and index.
ISBN 0-8239-4466-2
1. Nasser, Gamal Abdel, 1918–1970—Juvenile literature.
2. Presidents—Egypt—Biography—Juvenile literature.
[1. Nasser, Gamal Abdel, 1918–1970. 2. Presidents—Egypt.]
I. Title: Gamal Abdel Nasser.
II. Title. III. Series.
DT107.83.R67 2003
962.05'3'092—dc21

                                                    2003009382

Manufactured in the United States of America

CONTENTS

INTRODUCTION
AN EGYPTIAN LEADER

■ At age thirty-six, Nasser led Egypt's Revolutionary Command Council. Here, he is seen on August 1, 1954, making a public appearance to gain support for the council.

Although the Middle East is often thought of as "Israel and the Arab nations," this is not accurate. Each Arab nation makes up a separate country. Arab countries include Iraq, Jordan, Libya, Palestine, Saudi

Arabia, Syria, and Egypt. Each has its own principles and government structure. Egypt is perhaps the most distinct because it has undergone such major changes in the last century.

Egypt was a monarchy in 1900, ruled by a hereditary king. Its noble class held all the power, and the peasants suffered and starved. Today it is a centralized state, with an elected president. The government owns most of the major industries. People can find employment, participate in decisions, and own land. Egypt is an independent nation and refuses to be pressured by other powers when making its decisions.

Egypt's recent past has also shown two faces. In 1947, Egypt was the most vocal and active opponent against the creation of a Jewish state. For years afterward Egypt was Israel's most dangerous enemy. Then in the late 1970s, Egypt became Israel's only friend among the Arab nations. Today the two countries are still on good terms. What happened? How had this change come about?

Much of the change in Egypt can be traced to a single man. Gamal Abdel Nasser was one of the strongest Middle East leaders of the last century. Born to a poor family, Nasser rose through the ranks of the military. Then he helped overthrow the last Egyptian king. He eventually became president of the nation. Nasser faced down the superpowers of the world. He insisted on keeping Egypt independent from both American and Russian influence. He concentrated on making his nation strong again. He also worked to give the people more freedom, more wealth, and more stability.

Nasser helped carve a new path for Egypt and the rest of the Middle Eastern nations. He tried to bring the Arab

Gamal Abdel Nasser

■ Once a new Egyptian government was in place, Nasser worked to increase the wealth of the common people. Nasser knew he needed the confidence of the Egyptian people if social and political reforms were to succeed.

nations together and kept encouraging them to act as a group. He felt the Arab nations had too much in common to not work together. Nasser is considered one of the most influential leaders of the twentieth century. Not everyone liked him. Many other Arab leaders feared he would incite their people to revolt. The Soviets worried that they couldn't control him. The Americans worried that Nasser would turn all of the Middle East against them. And the Israelis feared that Nasser was the one man who could truly unite the Arab nations against them. But everyone, from his friends to his enemies, respected his courage, his idealism, and his dedication to the Egyptian people.

CHAPTER ONE
POTENTIAL

■ Gamal Abdel Nasser understood the importance of family and society for the strength of the Egyptian nation. Here, Nasser and his wife pose with their family on their twentieth wedding anniversary.

Great men and women often rise from humble beginnings. When this happens, they often remember their family's hardships. They struggle more fiercely to prevent others from facing the same difficulties.

Gamal Abdel Nasser was one such man. After becoming president of Egypt, Nasser spoke of his childhood: "I am proud to belong to this small village of Beni Morr. And I am more proud to be a member of a poor family from that village. I am saying these words for history that Nasser was born in a poor family and I promise that he will live and die a poor man."

Origins

Gamal Abdel Nasser was born on January 15, 1918, in the village of Beni Morr. Beni Morr stands within the Assuit Province of Upper Egypt. It is near the city of Alexandria. Nasser's father, Abdel-Nasser Hussein, ran the small local post office. He made very little money, but being the postmaster earned him a certain amount of respect. Gamal's mother, Fahima, also came from Upper Egypt. Her father, Mohammed Hammad, lived in Alexandria and made a good living transporting goods along the canals. The name "Gamal" means "slave" in Arabic, but "Nasser" means "the one who helps you win victory." Nasser was the couple's first child.

Life in Beni Morr was difficult, and the town had little money. The streets were unpaved, and most houses were made of mud bricks. People and animals packed the narrow streets. Filth was everywhere. Many people lacked work, and even those with jobs struggled to survive.

When Nasser was two years old, his uncle Khalil Hussein disappeared. Later the family learned that he had been arrested for organizing anti-British demonstrations. Nasser's father was terrified that his brother's actions would cost him his own job. He decided then that no other member of his family would ever get mixed up in politics.

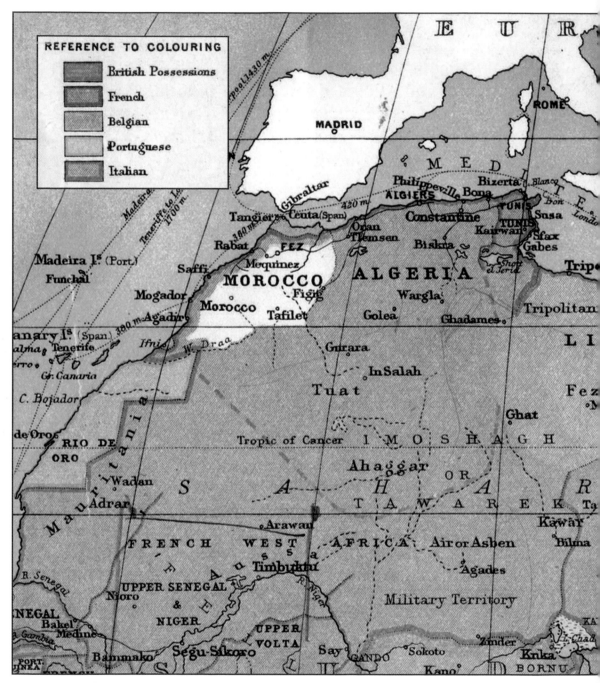

European powers ruled north African nations as colonies during the first half of the twentieth century. Independence did not come for these countries until after World War II (1939–1945) had ended. By then the colonial rulers had little money to keep up their military presence.

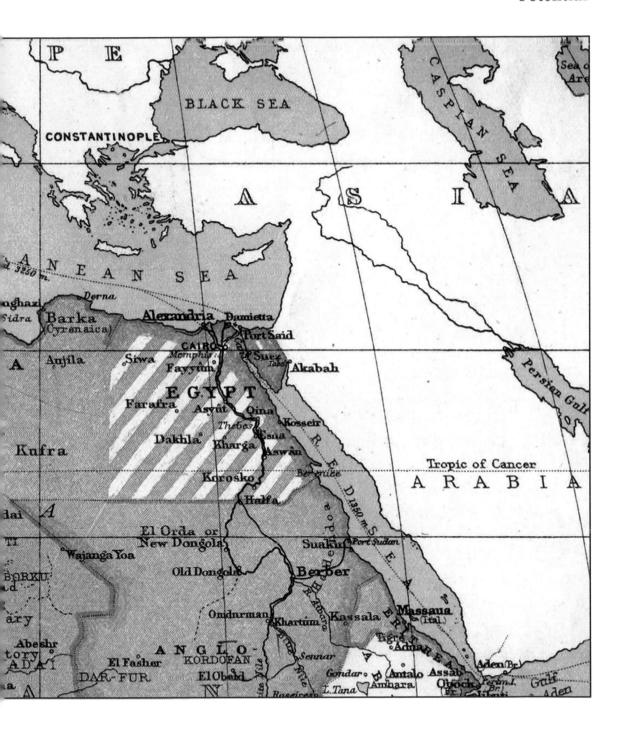

Gamal Abdel Nasser

By the time he was six, Nasser's family had moved to Khatatba. This small village was forty miles (sixty-four kilometers) from Cairo. Nasser now had two younger brothers. This was his first time living away from his village. He fell in love with the wide-open spaces and the fresh, clean air of the desert. Nasser went to kindergarten in Khatatba. Kindergarten was the only schooling Khatatba offered, and only the children of government employees could attend.

Education

When he was eight, Nasser finished the kindergarten course in Khatatba. His parents decided to send him to Cairo to continue his education. His Uncle Khalil was now out of prison and living in Cairo, and Nasser went to stay with him. This was his first experience with city life. He liked the variety of people and the constant activity. He was disgusted by the filth, however, and the poor living conditions. His uncle often worked late, and Nasser was left to look after himself most of the time. This forced him to become fiercely independent. He also learned to enjoy keeping secrets.

When Nasser was nine, his mother died while giving birth.

■ Pictured is Mohamed Aly Square in Alexandria, Egypt, in 1937. Nasser learned about city life at an early age. Such large public squares dazzled him. He experienced Alexandria's large crowds and busy bazaars, and saw his first public protest against British rule.

Nasser did not find out until he went home at the end of the school year. His father had chosen not to tell him. Nasser had always been closer to his mother than his father. Now he and his father had little to talk about. Nasser asked if he could go live with his mother's parents in Alexandria. His father agreed.

For the next three years, Nasser attended the Attarene Primary School of Alexandria. When he was twelve his father sent him back to Cairo after he did not do well in his studies. By this time Nasser's father was the postmaster at Suez. He had also remarried. Nasser had several half-siblings he had never met.

That summer Nasser visited his grandparents in Alexandria. One day he happened upon a protest going on against the British. He joined the group, having been raised on his Uncle Khalil's stories about British control. He wound up in jail with the other rioters. His father was horrified. He reacted harshly and sent Nasser to a boarding school in Helwan, thirty-two miles (fifty-one km) from Cairo. Two years later Nasser returned to Alexandria.

In 1934, his father, now at a post office in Cairo, summoned him home again. Nasser was sixteen. He and his father did not get along well. He also had nothing in common with his stepmother and his half-siblings. Nasser loved literature, history, and drama, but did not do well in mathematics or science. This displeased his father. The teenager began spending more and more time away from home.

He joined Misr al Fatat, the Young Egypt Party. This was the same extreme, ultranational group that had run the protest he had found in Alexandria, years before. When school started again he began organizing demonstrations, both in his own school (Al-Nahda) and in others. The party leaders disgusted Nasser, however. They were more interested in profit than in ideals. By the end of the year he had quit Young Egypt.

In November of that year, while taking part in a protest against the British, Nasser was wounded in the forehead. He refused to go to a hospital, afraid that he would be arrested. The wound left a permanent three-inch (7.6-centimeter) crescent scar. The newspapers mentioned the protest and Nasser by name. In retaliation against the student protesters, the government shut down their school. It was reopened a month later, although Nasser himself did not return until after his wound had healed. The protest had shown England how serious Egypt was, however. The British agreed to discuss restoring Egypt's full independence.

After graduating from Al-Nahda, Nasser studied law at Fuad I University. Even then, Nasser had dreams of changing Egypt for the better. He chose law because he hoped to better understand the rules that kept so many people poor and unhappy. Without understanding such laws it would be impossible to change them. Law was also a prestigious profession. Unfortunately, that meant a lot of young men were studying law, far more than could ever find jobs as lawyers. After a few months Nasser quit the university.

The Royal Military Academy

Egypt in the 1930s was a poor country. The British, who still occupied the land, claimed most of its wealth. Egypt's King Farouk and his court took the rest. Noble families grew richer, while everyone else became poorer. In such a

Gamal Abdel Nasser

■ Nasser *(center)* is shown here in 1940, carrying the battalion flag.
Even in his early twenties he showed a talent for leadership. During
his time in the military, Nasser's passion for and dedication to his
country won him the recognition he needed to rise in rank.

climate, a young man had few opportunities for success. In 1936, however, a new option became available.

The Royal Military Academy had previously accepted only young men from wealthier families. In 1936, Britain and Egypt signed the Treaty of Alliance. This recognized the two countries as equals and restricted British troops to the Suez Canal. This meant Egypt could increase its military and would need more soldiers. The rules of the academy were relaxed to allow young men from poorer families admittance. Nasser was among the first to take advantage of this new freedom. The military offered an opportunity for young men to advance purely through discipline, bravery, and focus. Nasser did not lack any of those qualities.

While training at the academy, Nasser finally had the chance to study without distraction. He focused entirely on Egypt and the Middle East, its recent past, the present, and possibilities for the future. His classmates often referred to him as "the somber cadet," but he was generally well liked. He met many radical-minded young officers, including another poor young man named Anwar al-Sadat.

Nasser spent most of his own time studying military history, tactics, and theory. Outside the academy he still spoke out against the British presence. He perfected his public speaking skills and his leadership skills. These helped his confidence and self-reliance. Nasser graduated from the academy in July 1938 as a second lieutenant in the Egyptian army. He was assigned to the infantry regiment at the Manqabad barracks in Assuit. His first military post was only a few miles from his birthplace of Beni Morr.

The Free Officers

While stationed in Sudan, Nasser began meeting secretly with eight other officers. This group named itself the Free Officers (El-Dhobatt El-Ahrar). They all felt that King Farouk and his regime were corrupt and wholly controlled by the British. Their goal was to overthrow both British control and the current royal family. They claimed this was for the good of the Egyptian people. Most people in Egypt were poor and working any job to survive. The king and his nobles, however, had more money than they could spend and owned most of the land. What money remained was being stolen away by the British, who controlled most Egyptian national companies.

The Free Officers knew this had to change. They decided the military would have to remove the king and take control. Nasser led the group, along with his friends and fellow academy graduates, Anwar al-Sadat, Ahmed Anwar, and Zakaria Mohie El Din. A few years later, while stationed in Alexandria, Nasser met and became friends with another officer, Abdul Hakim Amer, who also joined the Free Officers.

British Involvement

December 1, 1924: British tanks along the Nile

Egypt had been given independence from Britain in 1922. Britain had retained the right to keep garrisons and naval bases in the Suez Canal Zone. The Suez Canal provided easy access to India and to the oil resources of the Middle East. Britain had no intention of leaving the canal behind, since the country held part-ownership of the Suez Canal Company.

Even though Britain had no official control over the Egyptian government, British military commanders pressured King Farouk into passing laws favorable to them. The king signed bills that gave Britain more rights, more property, and more wealth. In 1936, the Anglo-Egyptian Treaty stated that British troops would remove themselves over the next twenty years, but this was not quick enough to suit most Egyptians. The agreement stated, however, that Britain could step back in if Egypt went to war, in theory to protect British interests in the canal.

■ As a captain in the Egyptian army, Nasser grew more bold. He had an intense commitment to the Free Officers and was the driving force behind their actions. In this picture, Nasser *(center)*, wearing a determined expression, stands among his fellow officers.

Teacher and Radical

By 1942, Nasser had risen to captain in the army. He was appointed as an instructor at the military academy. Abdul Amer became an instructor at the Army School of Administration in 1942 as well. This gave the Free Officers the opportunity to examine new officers. Nasser and Amer could also recruit any whom they felt shared their own goal of a free, independent Egypt.

During this time, Nasser married a young woman named Tahia. Nasser had been friends with her brother, Abdel-Hamid Kazem. He owned a rug factory not far from the academy. Abdel-Hamid was one of Nasser's few friends outside the military.

After World War II (1939–1945) ended, Nasser restructured the Free Officers. He divided the group into small cells and had Sadat create a civilian branch. The goal was still the same, however—to reclaim Egypt from British control. The civilian branch was disbanded in 1946, however, after it assassinated Osman Pasha, the pro-British former minister of finance. That July, the British removed their troops and equipment from Egypt, except for the Suez Canal

King Ahmad Farouk (1920–1965)

King Ahmad Farouk I

King Ahmad Farouk I was born in 1920 in Egypt. He went to boarding school in England before the death of his father, Fouad, called him back to Egypt at the age of sixteen. Farouk was widely regarded as a playboy. His rule was plagued with scandals. Most of Farouk's time was spent gambling, womanizing, eating, or driving expensive cars at reckless speeds. He tried to institute government reform but failed at each attempt, causing his popularity to sink even lower. The British also increased their control over him.

Farouk had supported the Axis powers during World War II. The British used this against him after the war. On February 4, 1942, the British ambassador forced Farouk to form a Wafdist government headed by Mustafa el Nahas Pasha. The Wafd Party was extremely pro-British and passed laws and resolutions to provide British citizens with more wealth and control in Egyptian industries (the Wafd members received money and shares in return). That was the end of Farouk's attempt to actually control the country.

Stories of government corruption became even more common. After Egypt's poor military performance in the 1948 war against Israel, Farouk lost the support of the army as well. Before that time, the Free Officers had nothing against their king personally. Now they blamed him for the army's poor organization and decided that he would have to be removed. Four years later, Farouk declared martial law to prevent the Wafd Party from gaining control. Instead, the military organized a coup of its own. Farouk was forced to abdicate (give up his power) and he left the country on his yacht. He never returned, spending the rest of his life exiled in Italy.

Zone. In November, Nasser was admitted to the Staff College, a two-year course that would lead to his becoming a staff officer. This would place him in a position of more power and control, and give him more influence over new officers (and potential Free Officers recruits). Nasser's first child, a daughter named Huda, was born earlier the same year. Huda's sister, Mona, was born the following year.

Israel Becomes a Nation

In 1948, Britain renounced control over Palestine. Soon after, the State of Israel was created through a United Nations resolution. Most of the Arab nations were angry with the United Nations for interfering in the region. It helped to give away land to the new Israeli state that they felt belonged to the Arabs. Arabs thought it an insult to Arab control of the region that the Jews be given their own nation.

More important for Egypt, America was helping to form the new state. Many felt this was in order to gain a foothold in the region. They feared American involvement would be even worse than Britain's had been. Many Jews were forced to flee to Israel because their Egyptian neighbors now turned against them. Israel also made a convenient target and helped distract people from problems in their own lands. The Arab nations, including Egypt, united to attack the new country. Nasser's class at the Staff College was graduated early, and he was sent off to Palestine to serve as battalion staff officer for the Sixth Battalion.

Nasser welcomed the war, but not because he was against Jews. His father had lived in a largely Jewish

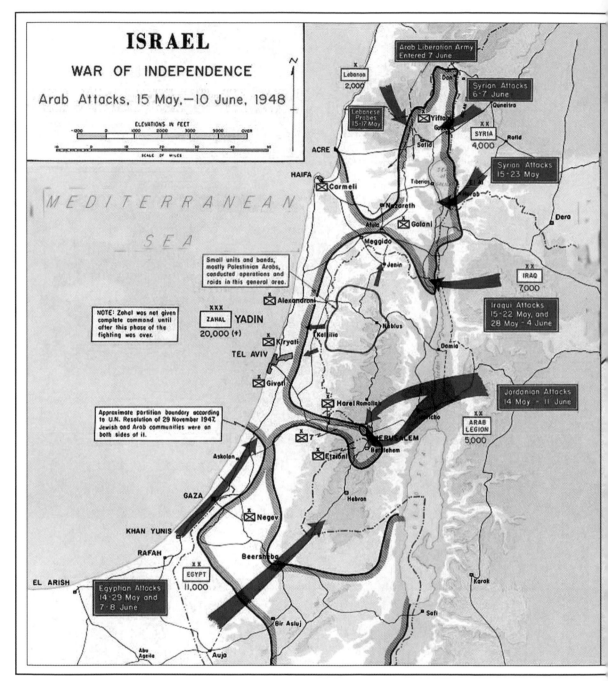

ISRAEL
WAR OF INDEPENDENCE
Arab Attacks, 15 May,—10 June, 1948

ELEVATIONS IN FEET
SCALE OF MILES

■ On the day Israel became a nation, armies from five Arab nations attacked from the north, south, and east. The map on this page shows Arab troop advancement and where and when the attacks took place.

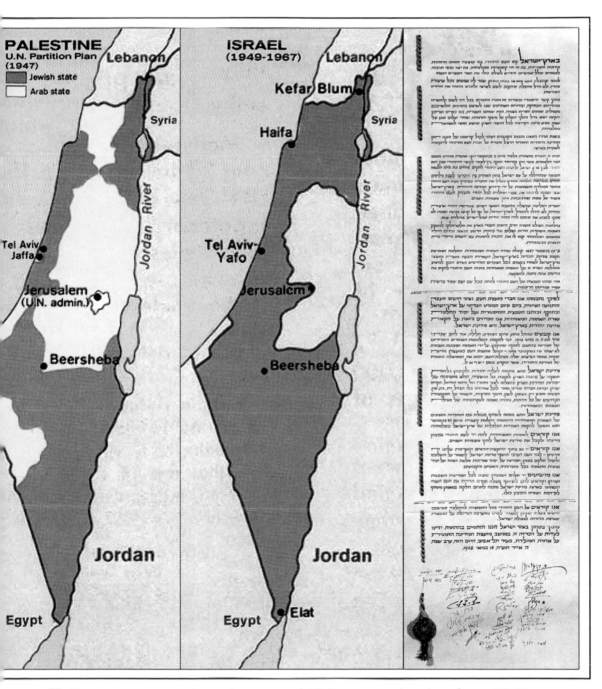

■ These two maps show the original UN partition borders from 1947 *(left)* and new borders drawn after the war *(right)*. The document on the far right is a photo of the original Israeli Declaration of Independence.

quarter in Cairo, and Nasser had no reason to dislike Jews as a group. Besides, Jews had been accepted in some of the Arab nations before this. But he saw the chance to give some pride back to Egypt's army after it had been treated badly during World War II. The war also presented a chance for the Free Officers to take control of military units and to gain the loyalty of their men.

Unfortunately for Egypt, its army was poorly prepared. It did not have the opportunity to coordinate attacks with the other Arab nations. Although many of the soldiers performed well as individuals, the Egyptian army as a whole did poorly. The entire nation felt a great sense of shame. Many blamed the king and the government for their failure, saying the army had not received their ruler's full support.

Nasser, who had commanded an army unit while in Palestine and had been wounded (this time in the chest), shared these attitudes. His battalion had suffered in October 1948 when Israeli forces cut it off at the village of Iraq al-Manshiyya. Israeli tanks shelled the village. The Israelis had not used tanks before this, so Nasser's commanding officer had chosen to

■ After WWII, the creation of the State of Israel proved a fateful turning of events for Egypt as well as other Arab countries in the Middle East. Pictured standing is David Ben-Gurion, Israel's first prime minister. He is shown reading the declaration of the founding of the State of Israel in 1948 in Tel Aviv.

■ Egypt's military involvement in the Arab-Israeli war didn't prove entirely fruitless for Nasser. He used the opportunity to solidify his relationships within the military and gain the support that was crucial to his future political career. Shown here in 1948 at Mount Sinai, Nasser *(bottom right, in uniform)* takes a break.

leave the unit's anti-tank weapons behind. Nasser had brought two anti-tank guns with him, however, in defiance of orders. With the two guns, the battalion held off the tank attack until other weapons could be brought up. The Israeli forces were finally repelled.

To Nasser, this showed the strength of his countrymen. He saw what could be accomplished when troops had strong leadership and a sense of pride. The battalion was later trapped for several months in the Faluja pocket, an area of the Gaza Strip about fifty miles (eighty km) south of Tel Aviv. It contained the Arab villages Faluja (or Falusa), Iraq al-Manshiyya, and Iraq al-Suweidan. Israeli forces encircled the area, creating the pocket and trapping Egyptian troops within this small area. Nasser was able to negotiate an agreement to get the men back out safely. He met with Israeli officers frequently. The two groups were able to talk with each other. This kept the violence from leading to personal hatred.

Israel called this Arab-Israeli war the War of Independence. The Arab nations gave it a different name: al Naqba, meaning "the catastrophe." Israel survived and signed separate cease-fire agreements in 1949 with Jordan, Syria, and Egypt. Israel wound up with twice as much space as the United Nations had originally selected, including most of what had been Palestine.

CHAPTER TWO
PREPARATION

■ Nasser *(seated, center)* is shown here with several members of the Free Officers. He knew that the only way to change Egypt's corrupt government was from within the military.

In 1949, after the war against Israel, Nasser was appointed as an instructor to the Army School of Administration in Cairo. He was assigned to teach logistics. This was partially because he had done so well keeping the Sixth Battalion supplied during the war. But Farouk and his senior officers had heard rumors of the Free Officers. They knew that Nasser might be involved. The army generals at one point questioned him. His rooms were searched, but Nasser never put any details down on paper. They found no evidence against him.

The Free Officers' Movement

Sadat and the other leaders finally convinced Nasser that the group needed more organization. The Free Officers formed the Committee of the Free Officers' Movement. In 1950, Nasser was elected its chairman. He was now a major in the Egyptian army.

The committee had fourteen members. Only Nasser and Amer knew everyone in the movement. Most people outside the committee still did not know that Nasser was the group's leader. They began circulating pamphlets printed by a friend outside the military to everyone in the military. The Free Officers used the military's own membership rosters as their subscription list. The movement had no particular political ideology—some members were Marxists, while others followed the Muslim Brotherhood (working to spread Islamic ideals). They all agreed, however, that both Farouk and the British had to be ousted.

The original Free Officers met quietly and discussed their plans and goals only with each other. It was too dangerous for them to reveal themselves until they had gathered more support. But the Free Officers' Movement was far more public and staged both rallies and protests, displaying its displeasure with the king's behavior, with Wafd policies, and with the presence of the British. The movement's goal was to gain popular support. This would make a transition of power easier and less violent.

The Free Officers were very careful. They incited riots but never let themselves be singled out as the leaders. Their pamphlets stirred up discontent and exposed many instances of incompetence and greed. The Free Officers themselves, though, were never directly involved. Farouk's men were desperate to catch the Free Officers, but they had no clues about the identities of its members. They could find no evidence against anyone that they suspected. Nasser proved too clever for them.

End of the Monarchy

By the early 1950s, Egypt was in terrible shape. The people were fed up with both the king and the British. The Wafd Party had lost much of its strength and reputation. In October 1951, the Wafd's leader, Mustafa el-Nahas Pasha, announced that Egypt was abolishing the Anglo-Egyptian Treaty of 1936. Riots broke out in the canal zone. Unfortunately, the Wafd found itself outnumbered and outmaneuvered by more radical groups like the Muslim Brotherhood. The Wafd leadership lost all control of the situation.

■ Perhaps one of the most vital aquatic shortcuts, the Suez Canal connects the Mediterranean and Red Seas. It stretches over 100 miles and can accommodate ships of mammoth proportions. Nasser was aware of the Suez Canal's political significance.

On January 25, 1952, British forces attacked the Ismailiya barracks in Suez. Fifty Egyptian soldiers died. The next day, Buluk Nizam, who had been in charge of the defenders, marched into Cairo with his supporters. He demanded arms to fight the British. Thousands of students joined the protest, which quickly got out of hand and led to hundreds of deaths.

In response to the riot, King Farouk declared the Wafd leaders illegal and declared martial law. What he failed to realize was that most of his officers were now members of the Free Officers' Movement. Farouk had just handed them control of the country.

On July 23, 1952, the Free Officers seized army headquarters and laid siege to Abdin Palace in Cairo and Ras El-Tin Palace in Alexandria. The next day, Anwar al-Sadat announced over the radio that, for the first time in 2,000 years, Egyptians once again ruled Egypt. He informed listeners that the Free Officers' Movement, under the command of General Mohammed Naguib, now controlled the nation.

Naguib had been selected as the figurehead of the revolution because

■ British soldiers look on at the Suez Canal in 1951. Buller Camp, owned and inhabited by the British military, was evacuated in 1953.

he was highly respected. His years of military experience lent more credibility to the coup. Nasser, now a colonel ("bikbashi"), was the real leader. At only thirty-four years old, however, Nasser felt he was too young to present himself as the nation's ruler. Naguib was a hero of the Arab-Israeli war and had been appointed president of the Egyptian Army Officers Club in 1951, beating out the candidate supported by King Farouk. This popularity within the army made Naguib the best choice for figurehead. His leadership ensured the military's loyalty.

On July 26, a military honor guard escorted King Farouk to his royal yacht, *El Mahrousa*, in Alexandria. He then left Egypt for the last time. His infant son, Ahmad Fouad, was declared king in his place. Young King Fouad was too young to be a threat.

Revolutionary Council

After Farouk was gone, the Free Officers had control of the country. They formed the Revolutionary Command Council (RCC) and asked Ali Mahir, a former prime minister, to head the government. The RCC also

■ Nasser *(center left)* and Naguib *(center right)* engage in a discussion at a press conference in 1953. Though Naguib was the first leader of the Egyptian republic, he fell out of the limelight shortly after Nasser took over the presidency. Naguib died in 1984 and has since been regaining widespread historical recognition as Egypt's first president.

removed all civil titles and instructed political parties to reorganize and remove weak and corrupt members. They elected Mohammed Naguib president and commander in chief. He was fifty-one at the time. The average age among the Free Officers was only thirty-three. They needed someone older like Naguib to lend them respectability and to help teach them leadership skills.

On September 7, 1952, Ali Mahir resigned as premier. The first Agrarian Reform Law took effect that same month. This limited land ownership to 200 feddans (an area just larger than an acre) and distributed excess land to peasants.

In January 1953, all political parties except the Muslim Brotherhood were dissolved. Political power was consolidated within the government. Naguib had no interest in making more radical changes, however. He also worried about the wisdom of putting military officers in charge of political matters. As time went on, Naguib and Nasser clashed more and more over their ideas of how Egypt should be governed.

On June 18, 1953, the Free Officers officially deposed King Ahmad Fouad and declared Egypt a republic. General Naguib was made its first president and prime minister. Amer was made commander in chief. Nasser became deputy prime minister and minister of the interior. This put him in charge of internal security. Mahmoud Fawzi, who had been foreign minister under Farouk, was asked to keep his position. Fawzi had no personal goals beyond service to his country. He did not even belong to any political party. The remaining British troops in the Suez Canal Zone were asked to leave. On July 27, 1954, the British signed an agreement to withdraw the last of their soldiers.

■ A crowd amasses in Opera Square in Cairo to protest British military presence at the Suez Canal. Opera Square gets its name from the Cairo Opera House, which is world renowned for its productions of *Aida*, an opera written by Giuseppe Verdi to celebrate the completion of the Suez Canal.

Around the same time, the council ordered Naguib to make Nasser prime minister and to have him form a cabinet. That had effectively ended any pretense of Naguib being in control. It had also ended Nasser's attempts to stay in the shadows and work through others. Naguib was still president, giving speeches and signing documents, but he was not involved in actual decisions.

Assassination Attempt

On October 26, 1954, the Muslim Brotherhood attempted to assassinate Gamal Abdel Nasser. They sent Mahmoud Abdul Latif, a thirty-two-year-old workman, to shoot Nasser with a revolver while he delivered a speech in the great square, the Midan el Tahrir (Place of Liberation). The attempt failed, and Nasser was not even wounded. Latif had to be rescued from the angry crowd by police.

The Muslim Brotherhood party was dissolved days later, after widespread public demonstrations against it. Its headquarters were burned to the ground by an angry mob. An investigation revealed a massive assassination plot. Each member of the Revolutionary Council had been targeted for death. Only President Naguib was to be spared. After more investigation, Naguib was implicated in the plans. He had been in secret communication with the brotherhood, and they had meant to restore him to full power.

Naguib was secretly tried and found guilty of treason. He was publicly stripped of office. He was not sentenced to death, however, as were the brotherhood members. Instead Naguib was placed under house arrest on November 13, 1956. Colonel Nasser formally took control of the government. Many regarded this as the true start of the 1952 revolution, for Nasser was not afraid to make drastic changes to Egypt in order to improve the lives of its people.

CHAPTER THREE
POWER

■ Here, Nasser gives a speech in 1956, shortly after being elected president. Egyptians were electrified by his inspiring speeches as well as his dramatic political style. Nasser gained wide popularity throughout most of the Arab nations.

Nasser's rise to the presidency filled several foreign nations with dread. Israel, of course, feared the notion of a vengeful neighbor with a strong leader. But Britain and France were also worried. Both nations had exhausted their resources during World War II. They now worried that Nasser might unite the Arab nations. If he succeeded, it would spell the end of British and French colonies in the Middle East. The outcome would significantly reduce the power and wealth of both France and Britain.

In fact, Nasser did hope to unite the Arab world some day. But first he had to unify Egypt. In a *New York Times* interview published August 1955, Nasser said, "I have read much about socialism, communism, democracy, and fascism. Our revolution will not be labeled by any of these names. We seek to meet the needs and requirements of our own people and we are not trying to copy anybody else's ideology."

On January 16, 1956, he declared Egypt a Socialist state, with a one-party system and Islam as its official religion. Every political party except the government-sponsored National Union was banned. The removal of opposing political parties helped Nasser maintain power and limited the chance of a rival seizing control. An election was held for the presidency, but Nasser's name was the only one on the ballot. He also confiscated over 772 square miles (2,000 square kilometers) of land from rich landowners. Afterward he redistributed the property among the peasants. The former landowners were outraged but were powerless to oppose the reform. They knew better than to try and fight Nasser, especially since he had the support of the military.

The Non-Aligned Movement

The Middle Eastern nations were being pulled in several directions, but the most tension was between the West (mainly the U.S., Britain, France, and West Germany) and the Soviets. Both sides wanted control over the area. They wanted its oil and a way to battle one another without actually committing their own militaries. Both sides were also concerned that the Arab nations, if they ever united, could become a major world power of their own.

Nasser, however, felt that Egypt had to make its own way in the world. Both the West and the Soviets offered incentives, loans, technical aid, and trade agreements. Egypt had only just won its independence, however, and Nasser had no desire to submit to foreign rule again. To keep either side from controlling him, Nasser played them against one another. He signed trade agreements with both the Soviets and the West, and let them compete for Egypt's interest. He refused to work exclusively with either side.

In April 1955, he attended the first Afro-Asian Conference in Bandung, Indonesia. Nasser met several other world leaders there, including Chou En-Lai of China, Josip Tito of Yugoslavia, Jawaharlal Nehru of India, and Ahmed Sukarno of Indonesia. This encounter with other new leaders helped bolster Nasser's confidence. Their success helped him believe that Egypt could survive on its own.

With Nehru and Tito, he created the Non-Alignment Pact. This pact stated that the countries involved would not let themselves be controlled by any outside power. They stated their independence and denied any alignment with an existing power, specifically the West and the Soviet bloc. This was, of course, exactly what both America and the Soviet Union had feared would happen. Historians agree that their pressure on Egypt was partially responsible for it.

The Third World

African traders weigh a bundle of rubber, 1943.

After World War II, many saw the world as divided between the Western nations and the Soviet bloc. These were considered the only two significant powers. Many simplified the division and saw it as the United States on one side and the Soviet Union on the other. These were considered the first and second worlds, in terms of technology, industry, and wealth. The term "third world" was coined to mean those nations aligned with neither side. Many of these were former colonies of one side or the other and had declared independence following the end of World War II. The term has come to mean economically less advanced nations in Asia, Africa, and Latin America, especially countries whose survival is based on trade with other nations. Today, the term "developing world" is now used to designate those countries that are less technologically advanced, have less wealth, higher rates of illiteracy and unemployment, and fewer ways to help and protect their own people.

The Suez Crisis

Even though Egypt was now an independent nation, British troops remained. Most of them were stationed along the Suez Canal, since that channel had been Britain's route to India. Nasser wanted the British out of his country. He began negotiations with them in February 1953. It took more than a year for the two countries to reach an agreement. Britain finally agreed to withdraw its 80,000 troops. Their agreement was partially based on the fact that India had become independent itself. Therefore Britain no longer needed quick access to its former colony. On October 19, 1954, Great Britain signed a treaty ceding the Suez Canal to Egypt. The treaty also required that all British troops be removed by June 1956.

The treaty contained one condition, however. If Egypt or a neighboring Arab state were attacked, Britain had the right to return. This clause was inserted by Britain to prevent the Soviets from taking over the Middle East. Britain also expected Egypt to join the Baghdad Pact, but Nasser refused.

Not everyone was happy about Egypt's new independence, however.

■ The British minister of state, Anthony Nutting *(center, left)*, and Nasser *(center, right)* sign the Anglo-Egyptian Agreement in 1954 in Cairo. The British prime minister, Anthony Eden, disliked Nasser and even to be in the same room with him. As minister of state, Nutting tried to create basic courtesy between the two leaders.

47

The Baghdad Pact

Leaders from England, the United States, and Turkey sign a declaration at the Baghdad Pact Council Meeting in London, 1958.

The Baghdad Pact is another name for the Pact of Mutual Cooperation between the Kingdom of Iraq, the Republic of Turkey, the United Kingdom, the Dominion of Pakistan, and the Kingdom of Iran. It was first signed in Baghdad, Iraq, in 1955. The United States and NATO (the North Atlantic Treaty Organization) created the treaty in an effort to build an anti-Soviet alliance. By signing the pact, each nation agreed to cooperate in security and defense, but also not to meddle in another pact member's internal affairs. This kept the nations united for a common good and assured that no one could force any of them to interfere with each other's domestic structure. Britain and the United States encouraged other nations to join. They were particularly concerned about Soviet influence in the area. By signing the pact a country could no longer attack any country that also had signed the treaty. Nasser was approached shortly after he took control of Egypt but refused to sign because he felt allying with the West would limit his country's options and keep Egypt from true independence.

After Iraq withdrew from the pact in 1959, the name of the pact was changed to the Central Treaty Organization (CENTO). In 1979, Iran also withdrew, and CENTO essentially ended.

Israel had felt that the presence of British troops would stop Egypt from attacking it without cause. Now those troops were gone, and Egypt was stronger than ever. Israeli agents had actually tried sabotaging the treaty talks by attacking British and American facilities on Egyptian soil (and blaming the Egyptians for the attacks). Egyptian counterintelligence agents captured and exposed them in 1954, however. This embarrassed Israel and prevented that nation from interfering further.

Having made sure that Egypt was now fully independent, Nasser began his next major project. He wanted to build the Aswan Dam across the upper Nile River, near the Sudanese border. With this dam, Egypt could irrigate potential farmland and provide more work, food, and money for its people. This was a massive undertaking that would require a vast amount of money. It was more money than Egypt had. So Nasser turned to the World Bank for help. The United States and Britain had agreed to invest in this project, and with their backing Egypt was approved for a loan.

Not everyone in America wanted the dam, however. American cotton farmers saw that the dam would increase Egyptian cotton production and cut into their own profits. They pressured the United States to cut its funding of the project. America was also angry that Nasser had officially recognized Communist China as a sovereign nation. Britain, seeing its longtime ally pulling out, backed out of the deal as well. Without the two nations' support, Egypt could not manage the loan. The World Bank withdrew its funding, and Nasser was forced to find another means.

Nasser was furious when he learned that both America and Britain had reneged on their agreements.

■ Nasser's bold decision to nationalize the Suez Canal put Egypt in the international spotlight. The Suez Canal Zone went under military law on July 27, 1956. Here, an Egyptian soldier stands guard at an office of the Suez Canal Company.

But he was not so easily defeated. On July 26, 1956, he announced the nationalization of the Suez Canal Company (Compagnie Maritime International du Canal de Suez). All tolls and tariffs paid by boats using the canal now would belong to the Egyptian government. Nasser planned to use that money to help fund the dam. He could also offer shares in the canal to people and nations willing to invest in the dam project. This increased Nasser's chances of finding investors. It also prevented the United States or Britain from blocking his project as easily. The former owners of the Suez Canal Company, who were British, French, and American, protested that Egypt had stolen their company. Nasser promised to pay them for their shares. The former owners protested to their own governments, who lodged complaints with the United Nations. Nasser then refused to allow international control over the canal. The situation grew even more tense when the Soviet Union sent ship pilots to aid Egypt in protecting its land. Matters continued to escalate, and the Suez Crisis had begun.

Invasion

When Egypt nationalized the Suez Canal, Britain and France were terrified. The Suez Canal was their fastest channel to oil supplies in the Middle East. Without control over that route, both nations would be at Egypt's mercy. The costs to ship the oil around Africa would have been enormous and hurtful to both countries' economies. British prime minister Anthony Eden wanted to attack Egypt. Britain, however, was not prepared for an outright war at that time. Instead, he contacted the leaders of France and Israel. The three nations began

■ Egyptian tanks enter Port Said after the final evacuation of British and French forces. Jubilant civilians celebrate the arrival of their military. For many Arabs living in the Middle East, the departure of British troops signified an end to imperialism.

plotting a way to attack Egypt together. Eden hid his plans from his own cabinet, however, and all three nations did their best to conceal the plans from the United States. Their concern was that the United States would object to their strategy. Israel began making small raids on Jordan. Nasser sent his commander in chief, Amer, to negotiate a military alliance with Jordan and Saudi Arabia. But the attacks on Jordan were just a feint. The real target was Egypt itself.

The final arrangement was for Israel to invade the Sinai Peninsula. Britain and France would call for an end to the fighting. They planned to threaten to intervene if a cease-fire did not occur. This would activate the clause in the original Suez agreement, since Egypt would be fighting with a neighboring country. This allowed Britain to legally enter Egypt to protect its interests in the canal.

On October 29, 1956, Israel invaded the Sinai as planned. Its troops quickly marched through the peninsula, taking Gaza and several other key areas. By November 4, Israel had occupied most of the peninsula east of the Suez Canal. Israeli troops made a point of targeting and

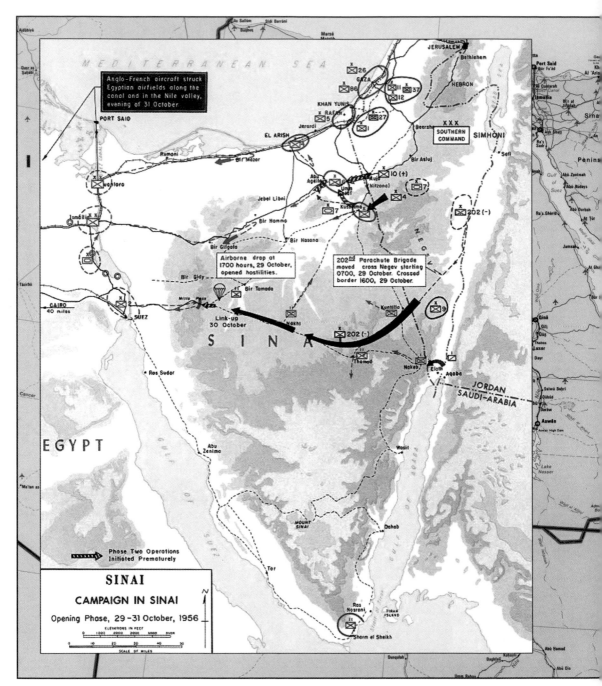

■ Israel's invasion of the Sinai demanded a fast, sweeping move through the Negev Desert *(map, this page)*. Paratroopers dropped into Egyptian territory on the afternoon of October 29, 1956. The 202nd Brigade moved south, then west to link up with the paratroopers on October 30.

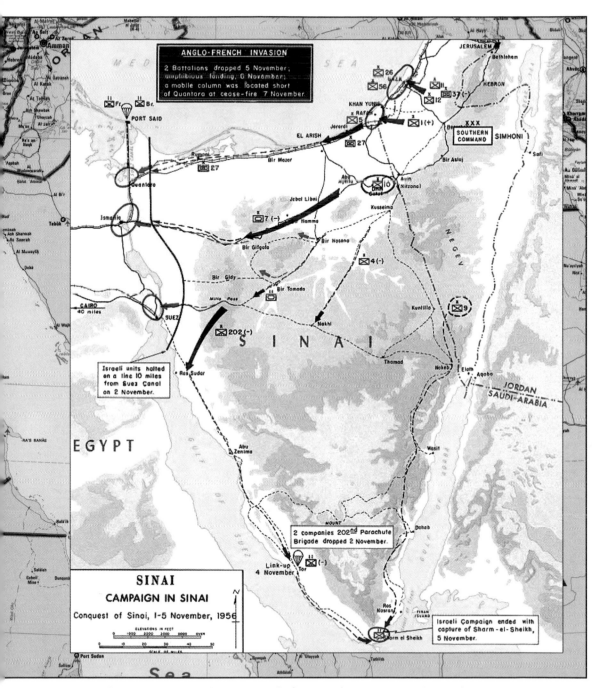

ANGLO-FRENCH INVASION

2 Battalions dropped 5 November;
amphibious landing, 6 November;
a mobile column was located short
of Quantara at cease-fire, 7 November.

Israeli units halted
on a line 10 miles
from Suez Canal
on 2 November.

2 companies 202nd Parachute
Brigade dropped 2 November.

Link-up
4 November

SINAI

CAMPAIGN IN SINAI

Conquest of Sinai, 1-5 November, 1956

Israeli Campaign ended with
capture of Sharm-el-Sheikh,
5 November.

■ Over the next eight days, Israeli forces drove west along three positions *(above)* and south to control the entire Sinai Peninsula. Israeli forces stopped ten miles from the Suez Canal.

destroying Egyptian bases. They wanted to cripple their neighbor's military power. Nasser gave orders for Egyptian forces to defend the country.

Britain and France had been prepared for these events. One day after the Israeli attack began, they presented their ultimatum—either a cease-fire was agreed upon by both sides, to be overseen by Britain and France, or the two nations would take steps themselves. Israel agreed to the terms, of course. It was part of Britain and France's overall plan. Nasser refused, however. The three conspiring nations had expected this. Nasser was proud and also angry that his nation had just been attacked. He had no reason to agree to a cease-fire when he was clearly the wronged party.

This refusal, however, gave Britain and France the opening they needed. The next day they launched air strikes against Egypt, bombing its airfields. On November 5, Anglo-French forces were landing at Port Said and preparing to advance down the canal. By this point the two nations had 22,000 soldiers in the canal zone. About half were British and half were French.

■ During a visit to the Gaza Strip, Nasser *(far left)* receives the admiration of his guardsmen and commandos. While he was there, Nasser placed a wreath on a memorial that honored Egyptian commandos who had lost their lives in combat during Israel's War of Independence.

Nasser and the World Respond

Nasser, ever the tactician, did not limit his response to military defense. Despite a bad case of laryngitis, he gave several speeches over the radio. In them he reassured the people of Egypt that he would never bow to foreign rule. He took personal command of the entire crisis. He directed not only troop movements but diplomatic responses and press releases. After the first air strikes, he nationalized all British and French assets in Egypt. He claimed for Egypt everything the two nations (and their citizens) possessed in the country. Unfortunately, this only gave Britain and France more reason to succeed in their plan. Nasser had now made impossible any other way for them to gain access to Egyptian resources.

Fortunately for Egypt, the rest of the world was outraged by the invasion. The Soviets threatened to attack Britain and France if they did not pull back. This forced the United States to condemn its allies' actions as well. America was not ready to fight the Soviet Union for this cause. The United States refused to protect Britain and France from the larger nation's military.

The United Nations helped deter a large-scale war by demanding a cease-fire for all parties involved in the Suez Crisis. Shown here in 1956, a UN vehicle passes some Egyptian soldiers at Le Cap. The United Nations was established after World War II as a method of combating such catastrophes.

America also worried that the Soviet Union might use this war as an excuse to increase its own presence in the Middle East. Such action would give the Communist government more control over oil and other commodities (such as cotton, grain, and lumber). Nasser knew the two nations would have to step in. He had appealed to America and the Soviet Union for aid when the attacks had started.

The United Nations demanded an immediate cease-fire from everyone involved. Britain and France, realizing they were outmatched, agreed to comply if Israel and Egypt also stopped fighting. On November 6 all sides ceased fire. The next day the UN Assembly voted that all invading countries must leave Egyptian territory. A UN Emergency Force (UNEF) was created and sent to ensure cooperation. The first UN troops arrived on November 21. Nasser was not happy about having outside military forces in his country but accepted it as a necessary evil. By the end of the year, Britain and France had completely removed themselves. Israel had returned all of the Sinai Peninsula except for the Gaza Strip, which it did several months later.

Victory from Defeat

The UNEF remained along the Egyptian-Israeli border and along the Sinai coast until 1967, to help maintain order. Meanwhile, the Suez Canal was reopened in March 1957. The canal was now firmly under Egyptian control. Relations between Egypt and Britain were now extremely hostile. Diplomatic communication between the two stopped. Links to the Soviet Union, however, were stronger. In fact, the USSR was regarded by many as the protector of the Middle East.

■ Pictured here is Mohimdar Singh, who was a member of the Kumaon Rifles from India. The Kumaon Rifles joined the United Nations Security Forces, taking positions in Port Said during the Suez Crisis.

Nasser had also demonstrated that Egypt could hold its own against three attackers at once. The Egyptian army had actually been badly beaten, but Nasser kept that information from the people and the press. Instead, he spread stories that their defeats had been few and their victories many. He became even more popular in the Middle East and was widely acknowledged as a strong political leader. Britain and France lost a great deal of prestige from their defeat. They quickly lost control over their remaining Arab colonies and allies. Israel's army had beaten the Egyptians, and the Jewish nation temporarily gained more land. A new buffer, the UNEF, now prevented direct attacks against it from Egypt. But in return, Israel had cemented its Arab neighbors' belief that the new nation was vicious and not to be trusted.

CHAPTER FOUR

PRIDE

■ Women played an important role in Nasser's Egypt. Women, like the men, joined the military and prepared for conflicts that might arise between Egypt and Israel. Here, the women are learning how to use submachine guns at a drill camp in Cairo, 1956.

One of the things that had contributed to Britain and France's decision to attack Egypt was the nation's arms deals. As early as 1955, Nasser had arranged deals with both China and the USSR. He gave them

Gamal Abdel Nasser

■ October 3, 1955: Nasser speaks about purchasing weapons from Czechoslovakia. At the time, Czechoslovakia was under Communist rule. Western nations feared the deal between the two countries would cement the Soviet Union's presence in the Middle East.

Egyptian cotton. In return, he received weapons and other military aid. Nasser was worried about possible Israeli attacks, of course. He may also have suspected that Britain would try to reclaim the Suez Canal. Britain had not made any threatening moves, but Nasser believed in being prepared. The military had overthrown Farouk, won Egypt's independence, and ultimately put him in power. To retain that power, Nasser knew he needed to keep the military strong and well armed.

Arms Deals

The United States and Great Britain did their best to control weapons sales in the Middle East. This not only made them money, but also let them restrict the type and number of weapons anyone possessed there. The two nations were also trying to protect Israel. They worried that Arab countries would use any new weaponry against the Jewish nation.

Nasser disliked being controlled. He also did not want to let the West restrict his options. In September 1955, he signed an arms deal with Czechoslovakia in order to get around America's restrictions. America claimed this as one of the reasons it backed out of funding the Aswan Dam.

Publicly, Nasser held Egypt to the Non-Alignment Pact and denied any special ties to any existing world power. Privately, however, his nation continued to trade with the Soviets. This business relationship helped build stronger links between Egypt and the USSR. Nasser had no particular love for Communism, but Moscow was willing to deal with him as an independent leader. It did not try to control Egypt the way America and Britain did. Nasser had

American Involvement

Nasser meets with Soviet leaders at the Kremlin, 1965

The United States government had very little involvement with Egypt. The American military had no troops in the area. American citizens, however, were involved in the Suez Canal Company. The United States simply trusted Britain to protect their mutual investment. As a nation that had overcome tyranny itself, America approved of Egypt's independence. It hoped that the newly freed state would ally itself with America and its other Western allies. American diplomats felt this would help offset any Soviet influence.

When Nasser rejected the Baghdad Pact, America was alarmed. It was unable to interfere, however. The United States became more concerned when Nasser began making arms deals with Czechoslovakia. This undercut U.S. control over weapons shipments to the Middle East. These arms sales, plus pressure from American cotton farmers, caused the United States to back out of supporting the Aswan Dam project. Ultimately, this decision hurt America far more than it did Egypt. Nasser simply turned to the USSR for funding and wound up forming a strong relationship with the Soviets as a result.

also become friends with Chou En-Lai. The Chinese leader had helped him build a relationship with Russia.

United Arab Republic

Nasser placed the survival and success of Egypt above all else. At the same time, he recognized that Egypt was part of the Arab world. Nasser was interested in cementing relations with his neighbors. He hoped that some day all Arab nations would have the same goals and policies. He wanted Arabs throughout the Middle East to achieve prosperity and freedom. He also felt that Israel posed a threat to all of its neighbors and could be dealt with best if the Arab nations united against it.

Nasser believed Egypt would be stronger if it were united with the other Arab nations. He also felt that the Middle East could and should become a single independent force. He wanted the Arab world to finally be totally free of colonialism and other foreign influence.

When Nasser completed Egypt's independence in 1956 by expelling the British and declaring a Socialist state, his fellow Arab nations were in no shape to agree on much of anything. Sudan had just become independent, as well, but had severed its old ties to Egypt. Morocco had also become independent but still had a king. Algeria was struggling to free itself from France. Libya was under the control of a religious leader, King Idris. Jordan was still partially under British control, though its King Hussein was fighting that. Hussein's cousin, King Faisal, ruled Iraq. Saudi Arabia was still controlled by its religious royal family. Yemen was a closed society, also heavily religious. Southern Yemen and Aden were still British colonies. Oman was facing civil war, with Britain supporting the sultan (Nasser threw his support to the sultan's opposition, just to block British influence). Lebanon was also torn between a Christian president and a Muslim prime minister. Only Syria, of all the other Arab states, was relatively stable, independent, and nonreligious.

This is not to say that Syria lacked problems. The Baath (meaning "revival") Party had formed in 1940. Baath members believed that the Arabic language and culture should be able to overcome any other differences. This group had some influence, especially over Syria's president, Shukri Al-Kuwatly. It did not wield full power over the nation, however. Also, Communist influence was growing, both in the government and in the military. Fear of a Communist takeover is what prompted Syria to approach Nasser in January 1958 about an alliance.

The Syrian leaders wanted a way to save themselves from foreign influence. Nasser saw this as the first step toward his dream of a united Arab nation. It was also a way to block Jordan and Saudi Arabia, who had reconciled their differences and were

■ Syrian president Shukri El-Kuwatly *(left)* and Nasser *(right)* sign an official agreement to join their nations into the United Arab Republic. The document was signed February 1, 1958, in Cairo, which was chosen to be the capital of the new state.

forming their own strong alliance with Iraq, against Nasser. Nasser knew he needed allies in the Middle East and needed to keep a strong, positive image. He proposed that they form a United Arab Republic (UAR), but stipulated that all political parties (including the Baath) must be abolished and that the army should be kept from interfering in politics. Syria accepted these terms, and the agreements were drawn up.

In February 1958, the United Arab Republic was born. Nasser was elected president by a vast majority (roughly 99 percent of the vote) and was hailed as a hero in Damascus, Syria. The UAR was divided into a northern and a southern region, with a single cabinet. Its vice presidents came from both Egypt and Syria.

UAR Opposition

One side effect of the UAR was that it frightened several of Egypt's neighbors. Those Arab nations with religious leaders, monarchs, and pro-West stances worried that Nasser's popularity would cause their own citizens to rise up in revolt, overthrow them, and take the nations over to the UAR. Jordan and Iraq, in particular, worried about this and created their own federation simply to oppose Nasser's ambitions. This angered Nasser, and he spent a great deal of energy attacking the two countries verbally and trying to overthrow both of their kings.

The UAR in Action

Unfortunately, what sounded good in talks and looked nice on paper did not always work in reality. Egypt had a strong political system and central government. It also had a single political party and one leader. Syria had been

Egypt's Flag

The modern flag of Egypt (1984)

In 1923, Egypt gained independence from Britain. One of the first things the country did was design its first national flag. The flag was green, with a white crescent and three stars in the middle. Nasser changed the flag in 1958, presenting a new flag for the United Arab Republic to symbolize Egypt's unity with Syria. The new flag had three horizontal bands—red at the top, white in the middle, and black at the bottom—with two green stars at the center. The red symbolized the struggle against British occupation and against the corrupt monarchy. The white symbolized the 1952 revolution, which overthrew the monarchy without bloodshed. The black represented the end of oppression. The two stars stood for Egypt and Syria, united as the new republic. After Syria left the UAR in 1961, Nasser retained the flag. In 1972, the stars were replaced by a golden hawk, which was also replaced in 1984 by a golden eagle.

fragmented, however, with power in several people and in various areas. Nasser's solution to this was to form a police force and let it and the army impose order. This had worked in Egypt, and he felt it should work in Syria as well. He did not concern himself with what the Syrians themselves wanted—Nasser felt he knew what was best for every Arab. Listening to too many opinions only diverted his focus. This was an attitude he had formed as a boy and had kept throughout his life.

Nasser rarely took suggestions and hated taking orders or having to explain his decisions. He had also begun publicly attacking Saudi Arabia, once a strong ally and still one of the strongest Middle Eastern nations. He criticized King Saud for his declaration that Saudi Arabia would never join any federation or republic. Iraq had gone through a regime change. The newly elected president, Kassem, expressed friendship toward Egypt but refused to join the UAR. Nasser was furious, since his people had helped instigate the coup and overthrow the king.

Unrest Within the UAR

Syria began to feel that Egypt did not treat it as an equal. Nasser did nothing to convince Syrians otherwise. Egyptians headed fourteen out of the UAR's twenty-one ministries. Cairo was the UAR's capital. Abdul Hamid Sarrai, the man Nasser appointed as Syria's minister of the interior and president of the executive council, was widely disliked for his strong-arm tactics.

Many people in Syria wanted to unite with Iraq. Iraq and Egypt, however, were now fighting for dominance. Since Kassem was a communist, this made Nasser attack the communists in Syria. This move angered his Russian

■ Yasser Arafat *(left)* and Nasser *(right)* share a refreshment together before discussing plans for war against Israel, 1969. The conference took place in Rabat, Morocco. The conference led to a heated argument between uncooperative oil-producing countries that refused to help fund Arab militaries.

allies. Syrian political parties were still operating underground. The Syrian people were also annoyed that Nasser's land reform and industrialization plans were taking so long to show positive results. Nasser seemed to ignore these problems. He was busy restoring relations with Sudan, Jordan, and Saudi Arabia, and devoted little time to improving his stature in Syria.

In 1960, Nasser abolished Syria's regional ministries and centralized the government in Cairo. This took away

■ Egyptians carrying an enormous portrait of Nasser gather in Cairo to protest the Syrian revolt, 1961. Many Egyptians felt that the Syrians had destroyed Nasser's vision of a united Arab state.

even more control from Syrian officials. He also nationalized their industries and introduced land reforms, angering the Syrian business community. In 1961, after a drought struck Syria, and Egypt provided very little aid, Syrian army officers seized control of the country. They declared Syria an independent nation and severed their ties to Egypt and the UAR.

The Aswan Dam

Nasser had not given up on his dream to build the Aswan Dam. He had increased Egypt's factories and industries. These improved the country's level of technology. The dam, however, would be another large step toward modernization.

After the Suez Crisis was over, Nasser turned to the Soviet Union for help with the dam project. He found that the Soviets were happy to help fund the project. They had expanded their link to Egypt and to the rest of the Middle East. Helping Egypt with a modern dam project would only help their stature.

Construction of the Aswan High Dam began in 1959, after Nasser had reached an agreement with Sudan. The dam was finished in 1970. It is

■ Building the modern Aswan Dam was no easy feat. Pictured here is the first stage of construction on the dam. The dam took ten years to complete; President Nasser died the year it was finished. Lake Nasser, a body of water that gradually grew from the dam's construction, was named in remembrance of the president.

considered one of the great architectural feats of the twentieth century. The Aswan Dam cost over $1 billion to build. It stretches 2.48 miles (four kilometers) across, is 3,281 feet (one kilometer) tall, and is almost a kilometer (one mile) thick. The Great Pyramid at Giza, another of Egypt's treasures, could fit inside the Aswan Dam seventeen times!

The Aswan Dam blocked the water of the upper Nile River. This formed Lake Nasser. This is the second largest man-made lake in the world. It is more than 300 miles (600 kilometers) long and in some places 25 miles (50 kilometers) wide. The dam increased Egypt's usable land to be irrigated and farmed by more than 800,000 acres (323,748 hectares). This acreage increased Egypt's food and cotton production.

The Six-Day War

Nasser still felt stung by Israel's victorious invasion. The presence of UN peacekeeping forces in the Sinai Peninsula kept Egypt from attacking Israel. Over the years, this grated more and more on Nasser. Nasser felt it was a sign that the nation did not fully control its area.

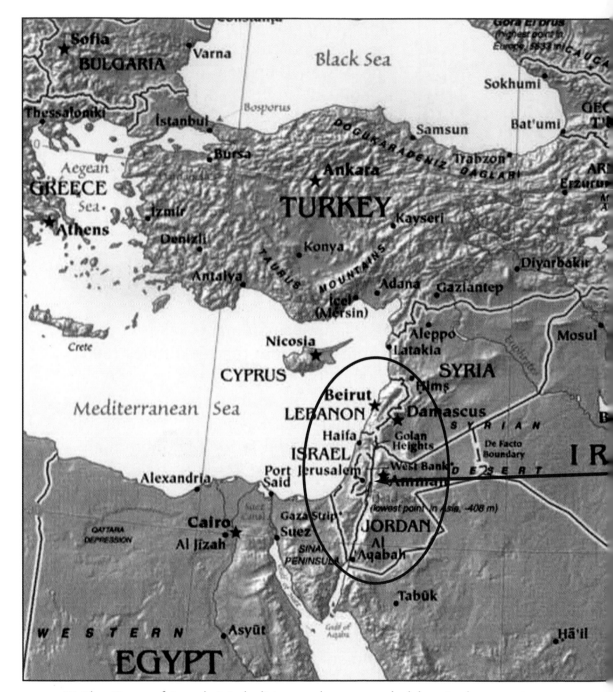

■ The State of Israel *(circled)* is nearly surrounded by Arab countries. None of the surrounding countries wanted Israel to exist. Yet the Israelis defended themselves well against every Arab aggression.

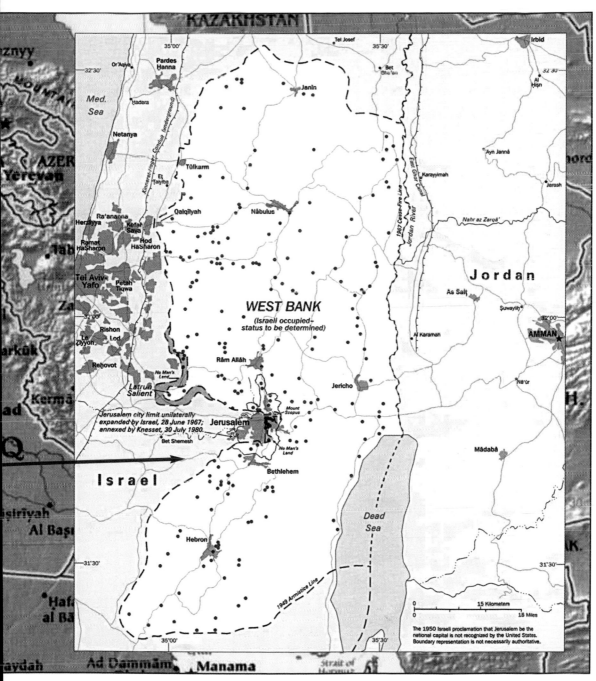

Nasser tried to regain Egypt's lost land from the Suez Crisis (1956) in the Six-Day War. Israel once again defeated Egypt, Syria, and Jordan. Afterward, Israel claimed Jerusalem and the West Bank *(inset, this page)*, and also the Gaza Strip, the Sinai, and the Golan Heights.

Nasser did not hate Jews, but they made a convenient target for the goals he had designed for Egypt. Nasser had focused his people's hatred against Israel to distract them from problems at home. He resolved to take back the land regardless of the United Nations. He communicated with several other Arab nations, and they united in their opposition to Israel. These neighbors agreed to attack Israel alongside Egypt, and plans were made.

On May 17, 1967, Nasser demanded that the United Nations forces be removed from the Sinai Peninsula. The UN actually agreed to this, and by May 22, all UN troops had left. Egyptian troops took their place. Then Nasser closed the Straits of Tyran, which blockaded the Gulf of Aqaba (at the south end of the Sinai Peninsula). This move prevented ships from reaching or leaving Israel's port of Eilat. Syria had already agreed to work with Egypt on the attack. On May 30, Egypt and Jordan signed a mutual defense treaty. A few days later, Jordanian troops mobilized on the border with Israel to assist in the assault.

Israel did its best to avoid open conflict. Its leaders tried negotiating with Nasser and other Arab leaders. They also asked the United States and Great Britain to speak on their behalf. They wanted the blockade removed, but Nasser refused to listen. Finally, Israel appealed to the United States for military aid instead. On July 3, the request was approved.

On July 5, the Israeli forces made a surprise attack in a move to defend themselves before the Arab nations themselves attacked Israel. Their first target was the Egyptian airfields. Israeli fighter jets succeeded in

After taking El Arish, Israeli troops head toward the Sinai Desert with Egyptian prisoners of war, June 1967. El Arish, an ancient, fortified village that predates the Roman Empire, sits against the Mediterranean Sea, approximately 200 miles east of Cairo. Throughout history, El Arish has passed between the hands of the Romans, the French, and the Turkish. Today, it belongs to Egypt.

destroying most of Egypt's planes while they were still on the ground. Egypt's air force was out of the fight before it got off the ground.

Nasser and his commanders had grown overconfident. Their forces were arrayed along standard Soviet lines. This setup used mobile armor units at strategic locations and infantry defending the border. They had over 100,000 troops and 900 tanks, in addition to artillery guns. But

■ An Israeli army convoy in Egypt during the Six-Day War. The Israelis astonished the world by winning a three-front war in less than a week. Historians and military strategists still are puzzled over the reasons for their stunning and unexpected victory.

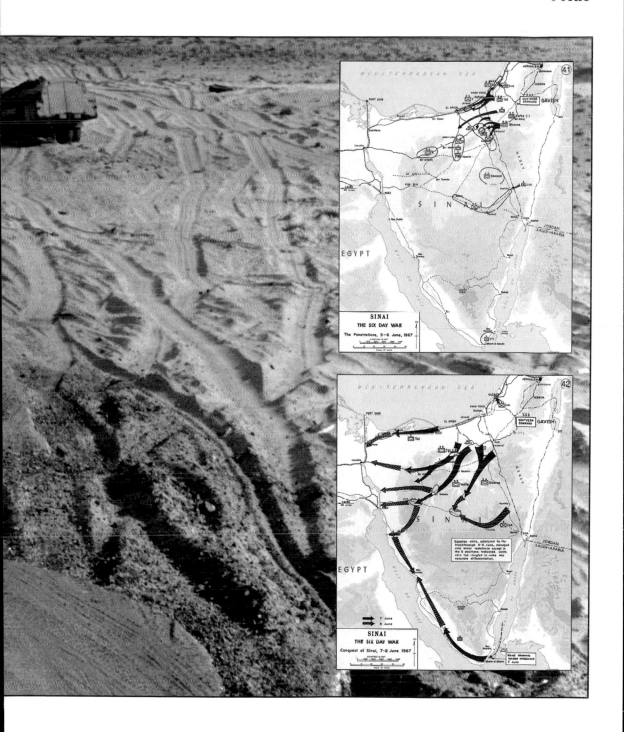

Ariel Sharon, commanding one of Israel's three divisions (as opposed to Egypt's seven), attacked the Egyptian infantry division at Abu-Ageila-Kusseima by encircling the area and then sending paratroopers to destroy the artillery itself. The Egyptian troops fled for their lives, leaving their equipment behind. The area quickly fell to Israeli control.

Egypt still possessed enough troops to stop Israel from advancing any further. However, the Egyptian minister of defense, Field Marshal Abdul Hakim Amer, panicked and ordered the retreat of all Sinai-based troops. Nasser, who had remained in Cairo to handle the rest of the country's affairs, was too far away to intervene. The Israeli forces hurried toward the mountain passes of West Sinai to block the Egyptians' escape. They only managed to seal the Gidi Pass before Arab forces arrived. On June 8, Israel finished capturing the Sinai Peninsula. That same night, Israeli air strikes destroyed two-thirds of the Syrian air force and forced the rest to retreat. The Syrian army was pinned down across the Golan plateau on June 9, and by June 10, the Syrians were fleeing. The Israeli air force also

■ June 9, 1967: Israelis cheer for their returning soldiers. By the following day, Israel controlled all of the Jordanian territory west of the Jordan River as well as the entire Sinai Peninsula and the Golan Heights of Syria. Approximately 1.5 million Arabs inhabited the land that Israel took over in 1967.

disabled much of Jordan's army, while Israeli troops captured the West Bank.

Nasser was unable to turn the situation around. He and Egypt were forced to accept defeat. A cease-fire was signed on June 11. Israel used its strong position as victor to control the Gaza Strip, the West Bank, the Sinai Peninsula, and the Golan Heights. The war lasted a total of six days, but in reality Egypt and its allies were beaten on the first day and simply hung on for five more days to save face. The Six-Day War was a grave defeat for Egypt. It also represented a serious blow both to Nasser's pride and to the image of Egyptian power in the Middle East.

CHAPTER FIVE

NASSER'S FINAL YEARS

■ Abdel Nasser and Aleksey Kosygin wave to the crowds in Cairo, 1966. Kosygin took over as chairman of the Council of Ministers of the USSR in 1964. He was the effective head of the Soviet government and shared his power with Brezhnev and Podgorny.

Though Nasser did not like to take advice, he was known to take the blame for his own mistakes. This was the case with the Six-Day War. Nasser felt that he had failed his people and his country.

Even though Amer had made the actual decision to retreat, Nasser had appointed him to handle the attack. Nasser decided that he was no longer fit to lead the nation and resigned as president of Egypt. The people would not have this, though. Hundreds of thousands of Egyptians marched in the streets, both in Cairo and in other cities (even in other Arab nations). They demanded that Nasser retain his position. Further, they insisted that the leading officers of the army were responsible for the war's outcome and should be court-martialed. Many politicians joined the marches, and finally Nasser complied with their request. He was surprised and pleased to see that the people still trusted him. In returning to the presidency, Nasser also became prime minister of Egypt. He had now completely solidified his power over the structure and direction of the nation.

The war had drained much of Egypt's resources, particularly for its military. To prevent being overrun by greedy neighbors or attacked by a vengeful Israel, Nasser was forced to accept increasing aid, both economic and military, from the Soviet Union. He attempted to rebuild the Egyptian army. Although it did grow stronger, Nasser was not able to build it back up to its former strength.

Nasser continued to work toward his goals of providing for every Egyptian and of making the country great. He had significantly improved life for most Egyptians. They had enough food, proper clothing, and decent homes. These successes had come at a price, however. The Egyptian people had only those personal freedoms Nasser felt they could handle.

Soviet Involvement

The Soviet Union sent military advisers and weaponry to Egypt beginning in the late 1960s.

The Soviet Union continually battled America for influence over other nations. Each country formed as many alliances as possible. Initially, the USSR had no chance with Egypt, since Britain controlled the country. Once King Farouk was ousted, however, and the British troops were sent home, the Soviets could approach safely.

At first, Nasser rejected any alliance with the Soviets. But after the United States and Great Britain tried to keep him from getting weapons, he turned to the Soviets for military trades. The USSR jumped at the opportunity. Now it had a relationship with Egypt, and it began to send other materials and goods to the nation. The Soviets also made deals to build new Egyptian industries. Egypt managed to maintain its independence until the Six-Day War ended in defeat. Afterward, Egypt was too drained to stand on its own. Nasser began to rely upon Soviet support and protection far more. This suited the USSR just fine. It gained even more influence over Egypt. The Soviets supplied not only weapons, but also soldiers and military advisers, to protect the nation's borders against Israel.

The War of Attrition

Nasser was a proud man. He had pride in his own leadership skills and in the progress his country had made since the revolution more than fifteen years earlier. He had held his country together, reclaimed vast areas of land for farming, increased trade with other nations, and significantly increased industry and technology. To lose the Six-Day War felt very much like losing the first Arab-Israeli war, and that made him furious even while it depressed him. This drove him to begin a new kind of war with Israel.

Nasser refused to leave Israel alone after the war was over. In 1968, Egyptian forces began firing shells at the Israeli encampments along the Suez Canal. Israeli planes attacked Egyptian areas in retaliation. This began the War of Attrition. Nasser knew that most of Israel's army forces were reserves. Such forces were only called up during active warfare. These people had other occupations and could not spend all their time fighting or defending from attack. Thus, he decided to attack slowly and steadily over a long period to wear down Israel's defenses and weaken its

■ During the War of Attrition, Israel shells Egyptian oil refineries in Suez. The war lasted nearly three years with over 3,000 military casualties and approximately 1,000 civilian deaths.

people's morale. What he underestimated was that every Israeli citizen was required to spend several years in military service. During those years they had no other occupation. The soldiers could devote their full attention to dealing with Egypt.

The War of Attrition lasted through the next year. Thousands of soldiers died on both sides, and nearly as many civilians were wounded. In August 1970, the United States negotiated a cease-fire. Neither nation was willing to admit defeat. The constant battle, however, had taken its toll on both sides. They were willing to set their weapons aside, at least for a short time.

Death Finally Comes

Nasser hosted an Arab summit in Cairo in September 1970. During the course of the summit, he attempted to solve the military conflict between the Palestinians and the Jordanians. The effort put a great strain on him physically. On September 28, he died from a sudden heart attack. Nasser's death shocked the entire Arab world. Millions of Egyptians joined the procession at his funeral. Gamal Abdel Nasser was only fifty-two years old.

■ Arab leaders convene at a hotel in Cairo in hopes of ending the civil war in Jordan between Palestinians and King Hussein's government. That day, King Hussein and Yasser Arafat agreed to a fourteen-point cease-fire under Nasser's mediation.

A Further Legacy: The Presidency of Anwar al-Sadat

Anwar al-Sadat, Nasser's successor, seen here in 1970

Anwar al-Sadat was one of the nine men who led the 1952 revolution and transformed Egypt from a monarchy to a Socialist regime. Sadat held several posts under Nasser, and in 1964, he became vice president. When Nasser died of a sudden heart attack in 1970, Sadat succeeded him as the president of Egypt.

Sadat was born to a poor Egyptian-Sudanese family in the Delta village of Mit Abu el-Kom in 1918. He entered the Royal Military Academy in 1936 and met Gamal Abdel Nasser there. The two cadets became close friends, even though they had very different personalities. Nasser was calm and patient, while Sadat was more fiery and always wanted to take action. Both felt very strongly that Egypt was suffering under King Farouk and under British control. In 1938, Sadat graduated from the academy. He joined the Egyptian army as a second lieutenant stationed in Sudan. Nasser was also stationed there. The two formed the Free Officers together. Sadat spent some time imprisoned by the British for taking part in a German spy ring, and more time for several attempts to assassinate officials. When he was finally released, Nasser put him in charge of the civilian arm of the Free Officers, but after they assassinated another official and were arrested again, that branch was dissolved.

Upon becoming president, Sadat took Egypt in a new direction. Nasser had allied the nation with the Soviet Union. That partnership was in rapid decline in 1970. The Soviet Union was not supplying the economic aid it had promised. Egypt was in danger of becoming a pawn for the larger nation. Many Egyptians had never approved of the partnership, including Sadat. Nasser's reasons to use the Soviets had made sense at the time. In 1972, Sadat severed the relationship. He expelled 15,000 Soviet military personnel and 5,000 Soviet military advisors. The following year, Egypt and Syria launched a surprise attack against Israel. This became known as the Yom Kippur War, and it demonstrated that Arab military power was not to be ignored.

In 1977, however, Sadat surprised everyone by visiting Israel and speaking with its prime minister, Menachem Begin. Two years later, the two nations signed the Camp David Accords, and Israel returned land to Egypt (and agreed to help establish Palestinian self-rule in the West Bank and Gaza Strip) in exchange for a promise of peace. The two men were awarded the Nobel Peace Prize in 1978 for their efforts. Many Arabs felt betrayed by Sadat's actions. On October 6, 1981, while reviewing a military parade in Cairo, Sadat was shot and killed by a trio of fundamentalist soldiers who regarded him as a traitor.

Nasser died poor because he had never bothered to hoard any of Egypt's wealth for his own personal gain. This was one of the many ways in which Nasser's leadership differed from that of King Farouk. During the monarchy, the king and his nobles cared more for their own wealth than for the people's welfare. Nasser genuinely put the needs of others before his own wants and desires, and had no personal greed.

Nasser's Legacy

Not everyone has agreed with Nasser's goals or his methods. Most do acknowledge, however, that Nasser was a great man and a powerful leader. He had completely transformed Egypt from a British-controlled monarchy with widespread poverty to an independent Socialist state that provided for most of its citizens. In a *New York Times* interview in March 1969, Nasser said "My dream above all is the development of the country, electricity in the villages and work for everybody. I have no personal dream. I have no personal life. There is nothing personal about me."

Nasser abolished feudalism and established land reforms. Impoverished

■ Nasser's death shocked the world. His funeral procession wound through the streets of Cairo to Manshiet-el-Bakry Mosque, his body's final resting place. Millions of Egyptians and Arabs crowded the streets to bid the leader farewell.

■ Nasser's sons, Abdel Hakim *(left)* and Abdel Hamid *(right)*, stand solemnly as Defense Minister Mohammed Hussein Tantawi *(center)* pays his respects over Nasser's grave. Nasser is still remembered today for his daring, charismatic leadership.

people received land parcels to enable them to provide for themselves. He nationalized the Suez Canal Company, built the Aswan Dam, and defended against attacks by France, Britain, and Israel. Nasser nationalized many of Egypt's major institutions and provided more work for his people. More than 2,000 factories were built during his tenure as president. He modernized and reorganized the Egyptian army. He also fostered Arab unity. This helped to bring many Middle Eastern nations closer together. Even though the United Arab Republic failed, a degree of Arab unity remains to this day.

Nasser was also a major international influence. He helped create the Non-Alignment Pact and form the third world. Egypt provided an example for nations refusing alliance with superpowers while still remaining able to thrive. Nasser himself was a major power broker and was instrumental in many alliances and agreements. He supported the liberation of other nations in Africa and the Middle East. People throughout the Arab world considered Nasser a hero for his success at freeing Egypt from British control and for the way he handled the Suez Crisis.

Perhaps Nasser's most significant contribution to both world and domestic affairs, however, was the restoration of Arab pride. For many years before him, the Arab nations had primarily been colonies of various Western powers. Western powers had dominated these poor nations—though they were rich in natural resources. Nasser showed beyond a doubt that Arab nations could make themselves great. He gave dignity back to the Arab world.

1918 Gamal Abdel Nasser is born January 15, in Beni Morr, near Alexandria, Egypt.

1924 Nasser's family moves to Khatatba, only forty miles from Egypt's capitol, Cairo.

1927 Nasser's mother dies. He spends the next three years at primary school in Alexandria.

1934 Nasser joins Misr al Fatat (Young Egypt Party) but quits by year's end.

1936 At eighteen, Nasser is accepted into the Royal Military Academy.

1938 Nasser graduates from the academy as second lieutenant in Egyptian army. He is assigned to a small post at Assuit. Later, while stationed in Sudan, he meets secretly with eight other officers. They call themselves the Free Officers and have the goal of overthrowing Egypt's king and kicking out the British.

1942 Nasser rises to captain in the army and is made an instructor. He now has influence over many officer recruits. He and the Free Officers begin looking for young officers who have the same ideas about taking over the government.

1948 Nasser is sent to Palestine to participate in an Arab attack on the newly established state of Israel.

1950 Nasser is a major in the army. His Free Officers creates a committee to better organize the movement.

1951 Wafd Party leaders demand an end to the Egyptian monarchy. Riots break out. The Wafd Party is outlawed. Martial law is instituted. This leaves the Free Officers in virtual charge of the country.

1952 The Free Officers take control of army headquarters and attack Abdin Palace in Cairo. The Free Officers elect Mohammed Naguib to lead the nation. King Farouk is deposed and leaves Egypt to spend the rest of his life in exile.

1954 Nasser is appointed prime minister. British forces begin to leave the Canal Zone. On October 26, Nasser survives an assassination attempt masterminded by Naguib and the Muslim Brotherhood. Naguib is stripped of office and Nasser becomes Egypt's president.

1955 Nasser forms Non-Alignment Pact with India and Yugoslavia.

1956 Nasser nationalizes the Suez Canal. Israel invades Sinai under secret plan with Britain and France.

1958 Nasser establishes the United Arab Republic with Syria.

1959 Egypt begins construction on the Aswan High Dam. It is completed in 1970.

1967 Egypt, Syria, and Jordan fight Israel in the Six-Day War. The Arab countries are soundly defeated. Nasser resigns his presidency in disgrace, but the Egyptian people demand he remain in office.

1968 Nasser dies of a heart attack at age fifty-two on September 28. Anwar al-Sadat succeeds him as president.

GLOSSARY

Aswan High Dam The enormous dam built over the upper Nile River. It is considered one of the greatest architectural feats of the twentieth century.

baraka Arabic for "luck."

Beni Morr A village in the Assuit Province of Upper Egypt, near Alexandria.

bikbashi Arabic for "colonel"; also the name by which Nasser was known (El Bikbashi).

El-Dhobatt El-Ahrar Arabic for "the Free Officers."

Gamal Arabic for "slave."

Misr al Fatat The Young Egypt Party, an extreme, ultranationalist group.

Naqba Arabic for "catastrophe"—the name the Egyptians use for the first Arab-Israeli war.

Nasser Arabic for "the one who helps you win victory."

nationalization Government takeover of an industry or area. That place or business is then owned and run entirely by the government.

North Atlantic Treaty Organization (NATO) A military pact between the United States and eighteen other countries, including Canada, France, Germany, and others.

Non-Alignment Pact The pact created by Nasser, Nehru (leader of India), and Tito (leader of Yugoslavia) in April 1955 at the first Afro-Asian Conference. The pact stated that the countries involved would not let themselves be controlled by anyone and were not aligned with an existing power, specifically the West and the Soviet bloc.

Revolutionary Command Council (RCC) The group of men, all Free Officers, who led Egypt after King Farouk was removed and before Naguib became president.

United Arab Republic (UAR) The Arabic coalition Nasser helped form between Egypt and Syria.

Wafd One of the major political parties in Egypt before the 1952 revolution. The Wafd Party had no unifying ideology, but many of its members were pro-British.

World Bank An international agency that provides loans to various nations for projects of self-improvement.

Organizations

American Research Center in Egypt
Emory Briarcliff Campus
1256 Briarcliff Road NE
Building A, Suite 423W
Atlanta, GA 30306
(404) 712-9854
e-mail: arce@emory.edu
Web site: http://www.arce.org

Egyptian Tourist Authority
630 Fifth Avenue
Suite 2305
New York, NY 10111
(212) 332-2570
e-mail: info@egypttourism.org
Web site: http://www.egypttourism.org

The Arab Organization for Human Rights (AOHR)
Cairo Office
91 Al-Marghany Street
Heliopolis
Cairo, Egypt
e-mail: aohr@link.com.eg
Web site: http://www.aohr.org

The Egyptian Organization for Human Rights (EOHR)
8/10 Mathaf El Manial Street, 10th Floor
Manyal El-roda
Cairo, Egypt
e-mail: info@eohr.org
Web site: http://www.eohr.org

Web Sites

Due to the changing nature of Internet links, the Rosen Publishing Group, Inc., has developed an online list of Web sites related to the subject of this book. This site is updated regularly. Please use this link to access the list:

http://www.rosenlinks.com/mel/gana

Brown, William F. *Thursday at Noon*. New York: St. Martin's Press, 1987.

Dechancie, John. *Gamal Abdel Nasser*. Philadelphia: Chelsea House, 1988.

Hobbs, Joseph J., and Charles F. Gritzner, ed. *Egypt*. Philadelphia: Chelsea House, 2002.

King, David C. *Egypt: Ancient Traditions, Modern Hopes*. Chicago: Benchmark, 1997.

Shivanandan, Mary. *Gamal Abdul Nasser: Modern Leader of Egypt*. Cairo: Samhar, 1973.

Stewart, Gail B. *The Suez Canal*. New York: Lucent, 2001.

Woodward, Peter. *Nasser*. London: Addison-Wesley, 1992.

Dowling, Mike. "The Electronic Passport to Conflicts in the Middle East." Retrieved February 30, 2003 (http://www.mrdowling.com/608nasser.html).

Halsall, Paul. "Modern History Sourcebook: Prime Minister Nehru: Speech to Bandung Conference Political Committee, 1955." Retrieved February 30, 2003 (http://www.fordham.edu/halsall/mod/1955nehru-bandung2.html).

Heikal, Mohamed. *Nasser: The Cairo Documents.* London: New English Library, 1973.

Koran, Bahgat. "The Arab States in the Regional and International System: II. Rise of New Governing Elite and the Militarization of the Political System." Retrieved February 30, 2003 (http://www.passia.org/seminars/96/arab_statesII.htm).

Love, Kennett. *Suez: The Twice-Fought War.* New York: McGraw-Hill Book Company, 1969.

Madsen, A. F. "An Overview of the Leadership Qualities of Gamal Abdel Nasser." Retrieved February 30, 2003 (http://membres.lycos.fr/transnational/luxorlad.htm).

Nasser, Gamal Abdel. *The Philosophy of the Revolution.* Buffalo, NY: Smith, Keynes and Marshall, 1959.

Neff, Donald. "Nasser Comes to Power in Egypt, Frightening Britain, France and Israel." *Washington Report.* July 1996. Retrieved

February 30, 2003 (http://www.washington-report. org/backissues/0796/9607083.htm).

Neff, Donald. *Warriors at Suez: Eisenhower Takes America into the Middle East*. New York: Linden Press/Simon & Schuster, 1981.

Nutting, Anthony. *Nasser*. London: Constable, 1972.

Shaer, Yahia Al. "President Gamal Abdel Nasser: A Life Summary." Retrieved February 30, 2003 (http://www.geocities.com/yahia_al_shaer/ YS-NASR1.htm).

Stephens, Robert. *Nasser: A Political Biography*. London: Allen Lane/The Penguin Press, 1971.

St. John, Robert. *The Boss: The Story of Gamal Abdel Nasser*. New York: McGraw-Hill, 1960.

About the Author

Sam Witte's family hails from Russia and came to America at the start of the twentieth century. Sam has taught college, designed Web sites, written book reviews, and worked as a camp counselor. His interests include history, philosophy, and languages, and he reads incessantly. He currently lives in Queens, New York.

Photo Credits

Front cover map, pp. 3 (chapters 1 and 4 boxes), 10–11, 22, 45, 78–79 courtesy of the Library of Congress; front cover image, pp. 1, 56–57, 64, 66, 68–69, 73, 74–75, 81, 87, 93, 96–97 © Bettmann/Corbis; flags on back cover and pp. 3, 4, 8, 30, 42, 63, 71, 87, 100, 102, 104, 106, 107, 109 © Nelson Sá; pp. 3 (chapters 2 and 3 boxes), 24–25, 33 (map), 54–55, 83 (maps) © Perry-Castãnedia Library Map Collection/The University of Texas at Austin; pp. 3 (chapter 5 box), 6–7, 98 © Corbis; pp. 4, 50, 52–53, 89, 94 © AP/Wide World Photos; p. 8 © Maher Attar/Corbis; pp. 12–13, 19, 26–27, 34–35, 36–37, 39, 42, 46–47, 58–59, 61, 63, 76–77, 82–83 © Hulton/Archive/Getty Images; pp. 16–17, 20–21, 28, 30 © Gamal Abdel Nasser/Al-Ahram; pp. 32–33 © Jim Pringle/AP/Wide World Photos; p. 48 © Hulton-Deutsch Collection/Corbis; pp. 84–85 © Vittoriano Rastelli/Corbis; pp. 90–91 © David Rudinger/Corbis.

Designer: Nelson Sá; **Editor:** Mark Beyer;
Photo Researcher: Nelson Sá